who
really
cares

who really cares

JANIS IAN

POEMS FROM CHILDHOOD
AND EARLY YOUTH

HAWK Publishing : TULSA

First printing 1969

Published in the United States by
HAWK Publishing Group.

HAWK and colophon are trademarks belonging to the
HAWK Publishing Group.

Printed in the United States of America.

LIBRARY OF CONGRESS CATALOGING IN PUBLICATION DATA
Ian, Janis
Who Really Cares/Janis Ian–HAWK Publishing ed.
p. cm.
ISBN 1-930709-37-4
1. Poetry
I. Title
[PS3563.I42145R4 2001]
813'.54   80-52413
CIP

PHOTO CREDITS
back cover – 1988 Carl Studna
cover – 1965 Merka Oser Fletcher
page 24 – 1966 Merka Oser Fletcher
page 42 – 1967 Peter Cunningham
page 70 – 1968 Peter Cunningham

PHOTO RESEARCH & SCANS
Tina Abato

HAWK Publishing
www.hawkpub.com

H987654321

I don't want to be a poet
I want to change your life

~ Rainier Maria Rilke

CONTENTS

peter

unpublished

The Problem with Poetry

The problem with writing a book of poetry, if you are a songwriter, is that you are a songwriter. You are not a poet.

At 15 I thought, excusably perhaps, that they were one and the same. It took me several years of hard work at my craft as a songwriter to discover that songs and poetry are about as alike as songs and chickens — both have their own life, and there is a natural order to that life, but otherwise they are very, very different.

All young girls write poetry, kept in journals hidden under the mattress, or in a little-used corner of their desks. The works in this volume are no better, or worse, than theirs. It was only published because, at the time, I happened to be in the position of having a recognizable brand name that would ensure some sales.

I was an annoyingly precocious child, of that there is no doubt. I started talking at seven months and, to quote my mother, "Never drew a breath since." Words have always been my safety valve, my way of understanding and connecting with the world around me.

When I was nine or ten years old, I decided I was going to be a poet. Not "When I grow up," or "After I finish school," but then and there. I didn't see much point in waiting.

It was complicated, because I disliked the poetry I'd seen. I found most of it stultifying, the rhymes labored, the images far too ethereal for the world of concrete and rock I occupied. My parent's bookshelves were full of the great poets, but none of them drew my attention. Reading words that existed without music, yet purported to be musical, made no sense to me.

Still, somehow I began writing, trying to capture what I felt on paper. Most of my efforts wound up in the wastebasket by my little desk. Once in a while I'd pen something I could stand to read the following day, and that would carefully be entered in my notebook. We didn't have a lot of money, and pens and paper had to come out of my lunch allowance money. From 5th through 6th grade I trudged home for lunch instead of eating in the cafeteria. My sacrifice allowed me to buy a Schaeffer cartridge ink pen every three months, and enough paper to keep me supplied. (I was convinced at the time that "real writers" only used ink pens. I was also sure they only wrote on one side of the page. I have no idea where those ideas came from.)

Since I was afraid to turn on the stove in case I burned down the apartment, I lived on tuna sandwiches and cold beans for two years.

The summer I turned ten I began playing guitar, and that changed everything. I decided to become a veterinarian, and be a poet, songwriter, performer, and recording artist on the side. It all seemed very do-able from the vantage point of East Orange, New Jersey.

I'd been stumbling through the local library, reading whatever I could stand from the poetry section, but it didn't seem very inspiring. To my way of thinking, someone who'd been dead eight hundred years couldn't possibly understand what my generation was going through. The arrogance of youth is astounding.

I got lucky one Sunday, when my parents took the family to New York City for the day. We wound up in Greenwich Village, standing around the fountain listening to budding folksingers strut their stuff. I darted in and out of the little bookstores, amazed at all the poetry books that *weren't* in my local library. Here was Leroi Jones, cutting out words from newspapers and making something brand new of them. Here was Ginsberg writing about the city experience, rather than the "dewy mists of morning rising o'er the sheltered hills" I'd come to expect. Here was e. e. cummings, putting everything in lower case — bold and brave and brand new, from the perspective of my sheltered world.

Here were poets I could relate to, people I could admire.

The discovery that I *liked* some forms of poetry spurred me to look again at the books in our neighborhood library, but to no avail. What did Chaucer have to do with the Viet Nam War? How could I take Shelley seriously when all he seemed to do was whine?

Unfortunately, none of the poets I'd seen that day were available at home, and I couldn't afford to buy their books. Instead I turned to biographies of poets, and ran across a line by Rainier Maria Rilke: "I don't want to be a poet. I want to change your life."

Aha! Light dawned. In addition to being a singer and poet, I would change the world.

It was the '60s. Anything seemed possible.

When I began writing songs two years later, I found that the words I couldn't fit into songs could become poems. The words I couldn't fit into poems could become songs. Since the goal of any brand-new writer is quantity, I was well satisfied with the arrangement.

Sometime during that summer, a camp counselor introduced me to two poems — *A Valediction Forbidding Mourning*, by John Donne, and *In My Craft or Sullen Art*, by Dylan Thomas. To this day, a copy of the latter lives in every notebook I carry. The counselor's patient tutoring allowed me to slow down enough to appreciate poetry a bit more, but I still found the vast majority of it horribly boring. I absolutely refused to become interested in the work of any poet recommended by my teachers. They were all dead, had been dead for decades or centuries, and bore no relevance to my life.

Then again, you must understand how much I hated school. Hated, loathed, despised. I found it insufferably dull, the teachers amazingly stupid, the class work tedious. Worst of all, it took me away from the piano and writing for eight hours a day, something I found unconscionable. One of the happiest days of my life was the day I walked out of high school, never to return.

Schools are not set up for people like me.

The classic poets I *did* begin to enjoy on my own were certainly nothing to sneer at — T. S. Eliot, Homer, Dylan Thomas (at that age I thought dying of alcoholism was very romantic) — but by and large poetry had no place in my life, unless I was writing it.

My family moved to New York when I turned fourteen, and I fell in with a crowd of pseudo-intellectuals. If I thought I'd disliked poetry before, I was now convinced I detested it. My friends dragged me off to "poetry readings," which were usually given by grim-faced people wearing black pants, black turtlenecks, and black berets. They'd sit on a stool in a dimly-lit room and intone to the masses, while everyone listening felt very superior. They were inevitably unhealthy looking, paler than snow, and convinced of their own importance to a degree I found absurd. I would sit in the back with my eyes closed, trying to appear deep in thought. Actually, I was catching up on my sleep.

By the time I entered the ninth grade, I was making my first record, "Society's Child."

By the time I finished that school year, my record was a hit, and I was working on my first album. And by the time I entered New York's High School of Music & Art for a miserable, ill-fated year, I was a full-fledged "star."

My management and other consultants became preoccupied with the thought that I should branch out into areas most pop singers of the time couldn't access — movies, television, books.

Remember, this was the '60s. Pop music was still very much "something for teenagers" — delinquent teenagers, at that. We weren't welcome at most hotels when we toured. Los Angeles' Hollywood Roosevelt

Hotel made my manager put up a huge cash deposit before they'd turn on our telephone lines, saying "All you rock and roll people welsh on your bills."

Serious musicians and serious writers didn't even deign to listen to us; we were considered too trashy and frivolous for them. Never mind that we were outselling their "serious" work by a margin of thousands — we were not real artists. We were just a bunch of pimply-faced kids who got lucky.

So the idea of branching out was a good one, both for my career and for the industry at large.

When Dial Press approached me with the idea of publishing a book of my poetry, I didn't want to do the project. I told my manager that I wasn't a poet, I was a songwriter. (By then, having put out two albums, there was some small truth to the claim.) But she, my agents, and my record company all believed this was a logical branch to add to my budding career. So the pursuit continued.

I said I didn't want to do the project for a full year, while an editor at Dial tried to convince me. When I argued that my poetry was inferior, he said he'd walk me through improving it. When I said I didn't know what I was doing, he promised that by the time he was through educating me, I would. When I said it was a stupid project, he argued that I had something to tell the world, and this was a way to speak to large numbers of the *intelligentsia* who'd never be caught dead listening to pop music. Appeals to an artist's ego usually work, and I am no different.

So I signed on the dotted line, and shortly thereafter, the editor who'd courted and wooed me departed for another publishing house. I was left with no mentor. To my recollection, Dial never assigned another "real" editor to me. Instead, I was told that I had to meet the deadline, which consisted merely of assembling the poems, re-typing them, and turning them over to someone at the company for typesetting.

When the book came out I was horribly embarrassed by the cover, a vicious shade of green with bright yellow and black lettering. I took myself pretty seriously back then, and I couldn't understand why my poetry book was being pitched toward psychedelia and head shops, rather than the literary crowd I'd been promised.

I'd thought it was my talent they were after. Silly girl. In retrospect, my naiveté is almost touching.

The book sold well enough, for a pop singer's effort into the literary world. The only book a pop star had published to that date was John Lennon's *In His Own Write*, so it was still pretty unusual. I remember that Dial were pleased.

I continued to record, write songs, and dither with poetry, but my world fell apart around me. I wanted to produce and arrange my own recordings, but 17-year-old girls were not allowed the sort of freedom one sees nowadays. My producer went on a three-year bender and disappeared completely, but the record company wouldn't allow me to conduct sessions in his absence, so I missed deadlines. My parents divorced, my career was in a shambles. Everyone wanted another "Society's Child," and I was incapable of writing a follow-up. I felt like a complete fraud. Hell, I wasn't even sure if I was cut out to *be* a writer, much less a *great* writer. And there didn't seem to be much point in devoting my life to something so laborious, if I couldn't be great.

Within a year of this book's original release, I was known as a "has-been," and a "one-hit wonder." There were even rumors that my parents had written "Society's Child." It was devastating.

I moved to Philadelphia with my boyfriend, Peter, and spent the next two years reading, writing, and trying to figure out what to do with my life. I discovered Arthur Rimbaud in James Ramsey Ullman's fictionalized biography *The Day On Fire*. I became wholly entranced with Rimbaud's life. I longed for *absinthe*, sure that it would provide any talent I was missing. (Remember, I was barely eighteen. Stupid, but understandable.) Rimbaud had said "The poet makes himself a poet by a long, deliberate disarrangement of the senses." I tried very hard to disarrange my senses, but it was difficult when the only drug that didn't scare me was marijuana. And it just made me crave spaghetti.

In between watching countless episodes of *Star Trek*, Peter began introducing me to the world of the intellect. I read Ezra Pound, James Joyce, Jean Cocteau, and found that I loved good writing. I devoured Camus and a host of other European writers, reveling in the language and soaking up their styles. I had no idea what, if anything, I'd do with it all, but I was sure I'd do something.

I kept a notebook of the poetry I was working on, alongside a notebook of songs to be finished. I really wasn't sure which one I wanted to devote my life to, but eventually I found out the hard way. Peter and I went to see the great runner Jim Ryan try to break yet another world record. I'd brought my poetry notebook with me, intending to do some work between sprints. Instead, I put it under the seat, and there it remained when we left to go home.

Somewhere in Philadelphia, a maintenance person may still have the thirty or forty-odd poems I was working on then.

With the loss of the book, my poetic plans hit bottom. At first I beat myself up over my carelessness. Eventually I realized that if it had been my song notebook, I'd never have left it behind. I understood what my unconscious had been trying to tell me, and set poetry aside for songwriting. And there I've remained, happily, ever since.

In retrospect, perhaps my "handlers" were wrong to push me into publishing this book back then. Most people don't have to spend their lives repeating the thoughts and feelings they had at fifteen. Then again, most people don't grow up in the kind of fishbowl I found myself in, with *Newsweek* and *Life* fascinated, and an audience of hundreds of thousands ready to hang on my every word. My management's enthusiasm is understandable now, from a business point of view. After all, what did one do with a 15-year-old "star" in the '60s? Remember, this is pre-teen idols, pre-Backstreet Boys and Britney Spears. There were only five of us who'd become stars by the age of fourteen; myself, Brenda Lee, the Osmonds, Michael Jackson, and Stevie Wonder. And as Donny Osmond pointed out to me, "You and Stevie were the only ones writing your own stuff. And you were the only one writing *real* stuff."

That was the problem with poetry, for me. I knew I didn't have the craft to be as "real" in that form as in my songs. Perhaps, if my advisors had realized how lacking my education was, they'd have seen to it that the deficiency was remedied before I attempted to take the literary world by storm.

However, also in retrospect, publishing *Who Really Cares* did ultimately lead to my conviction that I was meant to be a songwriter, not a poet. So the story has a happy ending, after all.

*   *   *

The poems in this book were written between the ages of nine and fifteen, and it shows. Some of them are wretched. Some are all right. A few are even passable, in a funny sort of way. But none, to my eye, show the sort of promise I showed a songwriter, so I guess it's a good thing my poetry book didn't revolutionize the world of verse.

Some of the poems were provoked by specific instances or people. *Like A Lonely Train Wreck, Sneaking* came as I watched Rod McKuen trying to defend his work during a television interview. I think I called it that because one of his books had the word "sneakers" in the title. Later, after I got over my elitist bullshit, I came to admire him for the simplicity of his work, attainable to one and all in a way mine could never be.

Cock Robin Is Dead was written for Native American singer/songwriter Peter LaFarge, who had always been very kind to me and whose suicide shocked and saddened all who'd known him. Death was still at a distance for me, but like any adolescent, I was preoccupied with thoughts of it.

Some of the poems were written directly from my own experience; most were written in the hope of someday *having* some experience. After all, however bright I was, I was still very much a child, occupying a narrow space between the world of my future, and that of my past.

To those poems we've added a number of others, which were unpublished until now. One or two were rejected by the publishers as "too much for our audience" (*I Read Sappho Before She Was Cool*). I think that was their polite way of saying that poetry about same-gender infatuation was not something they felt comfortable publishing.

A few of the others were "too personal; nobody can relate to them." (*Hate Mail In the Mail*.) While most people certainly don't receive razor blades in their mailboxes on a regular basis, it was a very real part of my life back then. Of course, the problem of biological warfare being conducted through the mails has permeated everyone's consciousness now, and the concept of a letter bomb is no longer as alien to most of us.

The world has changed a lot since I was fifteen.

There is only one newer poem, and that's *You Are Too Cute*, which slipped out while I wasn't paying attention one day.

There are footnotes to a number of these poems, to be found at the end of this book. When I was younger, I took great pleasure in appearing mysterious, mistaking inscrutability for depth. Now that I've gained a tiny bit of wisdom, this sort of posturing just irritates me. I've tried to place some of the older poems in context for that reason, and I hope it helps.

I make no apology for the work herein. It is what it is—the fumbling attempts of a child to make herself understood by, and to understand, the incomprehensible world of adults that surround her.

I've never had much patience; what little I've amassed, I've learned by knocking my head against a wall long enough to pass out. I expect that's one of the reasons poetry is still so hard for me to read. Reading poetry requires a suspension of time, and a willingness to enter into the author's vocabulary and syntax. I've always been too much an egotist to enter into anyone else's frame of reference that willingly.

I hope you will be more patient with me than I was.

Janis Ian
Nashville,
January 2002

jon

1954

Poems for the Young Bedwetter

one day mommy came home from the
hospital with a new baby
brother and she said isn't he
darling don't you just
adore your little brother and i said
yes but
when can we trade him in for a
newer model?

mommy says he is a
sweet little boy and
daddy says he is an
obedient little boy and
auntie says he is a
good little boy and
i say he is a
pain in the ass

teacher said don't you just
adore your little brother he is
always good   so
sweet and gentle don't you just
adore him and i said i
hate him

mom says little brother didn't
wet the bed last night if he is
dry tonight we will give him a
party with presents & cake
& candy & so tonight
i took a cup of water &
wet his bed for him

mommy says we still love brother
even if he does
soil the sheets even if he does
wet the bed we still
love him so
tonight i
wet my bed
too

jon

3

Horatio

Horatio sits
vomiting in a corner
The streets are hollow
save the pain of his laughter
soundless in agony

> *come off it, charlie*
> *fifteen an hour*
> *no more no less*
> *what's a body worth?*

His eyes explode in one direction
outside in, they speak
in red labyrinths
I enter slowly
afraid to touch too deep

> *and may God bless YOU*
> *sonny boy*
> she calls to the troop leader
> forty-eight and balding
> what does he care?

Looking at the overflow
drawers in his mind
jesus, it must hurt
to go insane

> *I can tell you stories*
> *Will you believe me?*
> *I can cry*
> *Will you wake me?*
> *I can laugh*
> *Will you love me?*

I tell the story
only too well
Can you believe me?
Will you believe me?

jon

The Droning Rebels

within the deep and misty caverns of the
"home james" politicians
who speak their gutters and whine
jungle jim and boy leap through the trees
in a frantic effort to recall
all the little puddles
suzy and billy
hide and seek
catch me if you can
and everyone laughs
even the prisoner

jimmy dean on his
motorcycle rampage and
kerouac the bongo player
gaze down from poet's graves to say
What's become of the younger generation?
angle-hearted hipsters of the
beat generation ask
What happened to the o so cool youth?
the tape recorders of the silent generation
think quietly (so quietly)
What has happened to the children?
but nobody really cares

london town is falling down
as the galleons of america invade with
pointed threats and quiet delinquents.
disciplined revolutionaries who walk
in a quiet city of dawn
to the insane asylum
and o it's spring again and
the whole world is
shit

Madison Ave. boys spineless
mindless lads with
dictated ideas
make great sofas
or foot stools
or tape recorders

jon

baby's down
shack town
cold green abyss
lights frantic candles as
elderly statesmen leap in the shadows of time
it's summer again
unaffiliated

elderly little old lady suddenly
runs to phone booth and
switches on her secret identity of
elderly little old man
everyone takes it calmly, talking about the
good
old
days every week they talk about the
good
old
days when they were
born they talked about the
good
old
days

snow falling white from sky as
Black Cardiac and New Lace walk to their
more favored café thatistosay the
Outsider where they find Square Cat sitting with
Hipsister and the FBI comes
Square Cat waves goodbye as they are
all given dehydrated seltzer for lunch &
subsequently you know die of
gas pains

oh it's summer again and the
pool is filthy as hell
dammit

jon

the sour little old lady crossing
all-saints boulevard suddenly
looked up and saw
god
being a religious woman she was
violently opposed to fanatics and
naturally went straightforth to the
police who came and shot god
d o w n
everybody knows real gods don't
bleed
christ

white snow falling gently into the
ribbon of the deep
heart of hate

jon

79th Street

Sunday night at the pool hall
i had an uncle tom
retrieving my ping pong balls
and each time i lost a ball
he bent to receive it

Somehow symbolic
behind the veneer and shuffle
i knew he laughed
much harder than i

Tears

hey — I'm crying, ma
my tears make hard salt crystals
they dissolve in my blood
and I cannot drink the cyanide
falling through this hollow heart

it comes quickly now
forming an icy wall
which slowly melts into oblivion
as once before, I stand
unclothed

hey! I'm crying here . . .
for the river of time is the bourbon and wine
my tears are of the cheap wine sort
the kind that comes in a carton
you know
or a screw-off cap

> *when you pass by*
> *and ask me why*
> *shall I deign to reply?*
> *what do I own but the tears of my song*
> *pray, let me show off my wares*

> and I say
> a pebble will outlast me
> a grain of sand for the mind of man

if you wish to see me as I truly am
come quickly
for I feel a kerchief
dabbing at the tears

jon

9

Poems for the Young Psychologist

i was going to take a bath
and mommy said don't
overload the tub don't
take too many toys don't
eat the soap
and the tub began to leak
i took too many toys
froze to death and
chewed on the soap
and when she asked where
did you ever get ideas like that
i said i just
don't
know

we went to stay with grandma and i said
o i forgot my lucky dog
mommy said dear its
old and its hair is
gone and anyway you mustn't be so
dependent
sleep without him
and i said well
you are old
and daddy still sleeps with you

one day i took a rock and threw it at mommy
& it hit the window which
b r o k e
daddy raised his hand to
hit me but mommy said don't
she'll get a complex
and daddy said sometimes dear you are just
too damned progressive

i was playing truck with jimmy when
daddy said she should play with
dolls not trucks
mommy said let her be she is
self motivated and he said
no and she said
yes and they argued
a lot
so in i went to ask for a
doll instead of a
truck
so they'd stop

we were eating when daddy came
home from a long tiring day and
started complaining how come the
food wasn't hot and the
steak was no good and the
house was all dirty and he
turned to me and
opened up his mouth and
i said
don't take your frustrations out on me
baby

jon

Cock Robin Is Dead (for Richard Fariña)

cock robin is dead
who wore a cloak of green
throughout sherwood forest
and stole the huac dream
cock robin is dead
who proudly wore his heart on shoulder
through the crazy splendor of a wounded
night
raining
he ran on a cycle through the forest
(just to see how far
was too far)
cock robin is dead whose
madonna wife asked him
why do you laugh?
and was answered
it's you who are laughing
at your reflection in me.
oh, yes, he's quite dead
in his black and silver chariot
he of amethyst and thyme
rode down a lonely road
the night passing outside
cock robin was a quiet fighter
and a hard one to beat

    Mmmm cried the mourner
    her sister with pale goddess eyes
    shone in the night
    like a chariot of fire

cock robin is dead
who wore a cloak of green
throughout sherwood forest
and stole the american dream
for a democratic one
    okay!
    (but don't cry yet)
the crucifix is just now being hung
and cock robin is
dead . . .

jon

Poem for the Christening

They sat quietly by the grave.

"He was such a good boy . . . always so polite."
The mother sat in silence
thinking of praise to show how sorry she was.
"Such a comfort to me in my old age."

Papa smiled
"He was an awfully good ball player."

And his almost best friend sat numbly
wishing he could leave but
not doing so out of respect for the grieving.

Papa suggested having all of His friends to dinner
and discussing their former good times.
Mama wanted to have the relatives over
and speak of His past life —
the things that were important to Him.
(bar mitzvah, first day in school, and other
like necessities.)
She smiled and asked if perhaps they might
have a small gathering . . . uh, a quiet party
one might say.
In His honor,
of course,
I'm sure He would have wanted it that way,
she said, it would be nice.

Not that we really want to see the relatives,
mused Papa,
but just the same
it would be nice.

And his almost best friend replied
"Let's all of us go home and
everyone remember by themselves.
No parties.
Just carry on."
Which was, of course, exactly
the way
he'd have wanted it.

jon

Philo Judaeus

The river tide is run
Philo Judaeus
Your shaken bowl
cannot hold the earth

> No more
> > the eyes of God intone
> > Halt the slaughter of angels .
>
> No more yesterdays
> > written plain on parchment
>
> Our kingdom come
> does not exist
> for the likes of us

> No more loving mothers
> > Philo Judaeus
> > we have been forgotten
>
> Never mind the ecstasy
> Hide your sailor's eyes
> > they can not save us

Philo Judaeus
imagine

No more
> you
No more
> me

Even God is weeping

Mandy In Mourning

Mandy
sits in a chair
legs in the air
neither here nor there

> She would never hurt you
> Wouldn't even touch a fly
> but nobody believes her
> and no one receives her
> She would welcome you
> with open eyes
> offering bread and butter
> outhouse shelter
> helter skelter

> They say
>   she lives
>   in a fantasy world

Mandy's
playing games
no sense of shame
and who's to blame?

Folks say it's a disgrace
but she's not listening

I would tell her mother
but I couldn't breathe a word of it
to Mandy

> whose eyes overflow
> in shiny salt seas
> and all she ever wanted
> was to be like you and me

jon

15

Epitaph

when the cyclone winds took
air and slapped the sand
        right into
                arab's
                        face

when the heaviest sun
added weight to a
        prisoner's
                shovel and
                        pick

when the poverty came
and choked just like a
        poor man's
                starched
                        collar

jesus had come again
stoned for impersonation
        and sat
                upon the
                        open air

Who Comes So Lonely In The Night?

My laughter is the joyfilled hysteria of one
who laughs to avoid the snapping of his mind
> (Listen to the sound of one room, ticking)

My shame is the shame of a madman
sorrowed on seeing what he could not help but do
> (Listen to the silence of my song)

My illness is that of the patient who,
on seeing how little time is left,
must needs get it all done quickly
> (You are not deaf
> There is nothing to hear)

My words are the words of one
who has forgotten his native tongue
> (Listen to the language of our eyes)

My poems are those of a man on an island
seeking to recapture what once he knew
> (Listen to the rustle of dead leaves)

My songs are those of the swallow who
caught in a web, imprisoned 'til death,
sings only that he may not be forgotten
> (Watch the gannet in flight,
> How quickly he falls)

My wishes are those of a prisoner
who sees what he can no longer have
and only yearns for it all the more
> (Listen for the sound of a wish on a star
> How many stars before a wish can shatter?)

My wants are those of a human
My life is that of a half-woman
And my tears are those of one
who has nothing left to give
but sorrow

jon

With His Crazy Black Hair, Whistling A Breeze

So now he's gone from my life
Of his own free will he left — he did
with his crazy black hair flapping in the breeze
as it did when he used to tease
and pretend he was going but
this time, there's no pretending

"He was so bright!"
Stunned, they were
but there's no time for genius
when you have problems to solve
and crazy black hair to wave in the breeze

Who wiped your tears away?
Who heard you cry?
Who put the knife of hate
into so young a heart?

No . . .
Not I
who loved you more than yesterday
respected in the same.
Not I.

Who'll give their time to love,
when there are problems to be solved
and crazy black hair to wave in the breeze?

And how will you fare without the breeze
my love?

jon

Mama & me

O mama
I'm bleeding
And you stop up my wounds with cyanide
        you grabbed from my dreams
        each night
        as I lay there
        thinking of you

O mama
I'm hurting
And you soothe the tears with
smoke in my eyes
        the smoke you steal
        from the incense I burn
        in filial devotion

O mama
I'm burning
And you cool my brow with
rags dipped in kerosene
        and you take the rags
        from the sackcloth I wear
        to remind me of you

O mama
I'm dying
And I'll cool your brow
        with my spit
And I'll soothe your wounds
        with my fists
And I'll stop up your tears
        with laughter

O mama
And when the end comes
shall we tell them what it means
to interrupt a dream?

jon

Letter to the Damned

Year of their lord, soon to be designed
in a pattern of the mind
so much less than rhyme

The second stage having begun,
Jeffrey the Pumpkin Maker
wandered out of his car forcefully.
'What did you learn in school?'
asked the high priestess.

'Ho boy' replied Jeffrey atavistically.
'If the moon were not so high
I should become an activist.'

'This is something new' said father,
sipping from a genuine tea glass of imported japan.
'Possibly just a face he's going through.'

'Jeffrey laughed with scorn' said the high priestess.

Jeffrey laughed with scorn and replied 'Not so
not so. How long is it since you've seen Jeremiah
. . . or even an angel?'

Finding no reply, he trundled to the car
and turned his back on the future.

Jeffrey the Pumpkin Maker died of eating too many
humanoids next week. The high priestess was
coveted and father left for the mountains to become
a guru. Myself, I wish for Jeffrey the best of luck
and relief from tension or sin.

Hoping you're the same . . .

jon

20

Jon

Once, Jon, I could have told you
>   why the nightbird flew by day
>   and winter flowers bloomed in may
>   and people always seemed to speak
>   when they had nothing to say

But hey, Jon — I've grown
too young to sit and cry
too small to wonder why
All I do today is sit
and laugh the hurt away

>   Only
>   let me laugh a little longer

Once, Jon, I could have told you
>   why open avenues of sound
>   closed all about you
>   and "accidental" bullets always found you
>   and none of the cheating do-you-inners
>   ever had need to doubt you
>   The lonely island man could always find you

Once, Jon, I could have shown you
>   why women only cried a child's tears
>   and laughing boys never felt the fear
>   and we weren't deaf, there was
>   nothing left to hear
>   and all of us would live to face another year

But hey, Jon — I've grown too young
to try and explain
Too small to push away the pain
And all I do today is laugh
the hurting times away

>   God
>   if you'd just have laughed a little longer

new york

1966

Shaving the Turkey

Don't kid yourself
Reality is their excuse
For anything unpleasant

> for war
> and hate
> and riots
> and newark

Go out and hop a train
Pay your dues
Thirsty boots
Oh for the glory of a depression

> when everyone lived the dream
> of better days to come

Affluent is what we are
Rich as hell and probably
we'll die that way
With a little luck
I'll go to heaven
and start a rebellion

> or possibly they, too, have a statute
> forbidding advocating the
> violent overthrow of
> government

> I wonder if God has any
> interior motive

Everything is realized in the night these days
The day succeeds the night

> which succeeds in
> making a fool of itself
> And I myself succeed the day
> ha
> ha
> I'm drowning

Poem for a Guidance Counselor

teacher said do you
hate your mommy? i said i
love her and she said you're
lying you don't really
mean that
do you?
i said i'm sorry i
love her and she said i was
very
sick

Lighthouse

I live in the country of the blind
They call me "gifted"
with sight
Yet their hands move faster
than the eye can see

I live in a country of the blind
but my room is darkest of them all

Through These Hallowed Halls

In mourning
at sunset
we make our way

> through these hallowed halls
> I've been
> searching for the end
>> boys in blue ribbon
>> surrender my cause

The trees
are weeping
can't you see?

> sunlight through my hollow prism
> yes, I face the park
> and keep my eyes downcast
>> not to be bothered
>> by spring

Let me ride!
I'll break the walls
nervous tutor

> yesterday the sun was high
> today it's all in shadows
> would you like to keep me here
>> a useful member
>> of society?

I should fly to the heights
of your misery
locked in too long
> no wonder I carry
> a knife

>> far better to be swallowed
>> by the sun
>> than wallow in darkness
>> forever

new york

Eugene the Crazyboy

Hey it's Eugene the Crazyboy!
I wonder is it all an act?
Everyone treats him like thin glass
Don't shout—you'll break it!
Me, I treat him like I do my friends
Don't break — I'm shouting!

Eugene doesn't talk so good with strangers
Gives them weird answers or just
doesn't answer at all
And they think it's absurd

> He talks real good to me, though
> Always smiles. We talk
> about horses and government
> and swimming and living and
> just about anything we think of

> But when anyone else comes by
> he stutters to a stop

Eugene gave me a present
A clip-on earring
And I said   Thank you
putting it in my pants
just to prove the point
He wanted it back
later

Eugene the Crazyboy got put away
in a home with sterilized nurses
with an official insanity card
But I'll bet you a fiver
he never gives them presents

new york

Aesop's Fables

I am no stranger to tears
My life flows by
The rivers cry
As I die
>hoping that my makeup
>will cover up the fear
>hoping my new clothing
>will keep away the tears

Saying to you 'Oh nothing, really
there's too much smoke in here'
As I creep off to powder my nose
at the party
>I am no stranger to lonely
>Sitting in my one-celled room
>Waiting for the nightly doom
>to take me
>>wishing I had time to think
>>about the world of time
>>wishing I had time to blink
>>and stop, for just a while

As I crawl behind the jukebox
of a restaurant
>I am no stranger to fear
>Walking through the rain
>Stumbling toward a train
>Take me away
>>praying that my terror
>>will hide itself in darkness
>>praying that my horror
>>will think it's only loneliness

Creeping toward the moon
and coming home
>Yes but I am a stranger to love
>Sit in the room, hugging my knees
>Laughter shines at memories
>you bring to me
>>hoping for the sunlight
>>to smile at me through dawn
>>hoping for the shadows
>>to take your place and form

Crawling from my room
and to your bedside

new york

30

Hunter

So die a slow death
Hunter
Indian warriors will sing your anthem
over the burial ashes
We will send you off
all silver and gold
Rubies in your hand
And a smile upon your face
for all the secrets we'll never know

A Chess Player

The aged are our dearest friends
for only they may teach us
        to comply; with gratitude
the weary soul, bereft of man
        stumbles once again.

        Someday, shall I live forever?
                (weakness of the flesh)
        I envy not the setting sun
                for rising once again.
        Never having had the time
                to own a memory,
        I see my soul a living shell
                of dubious quality.

To meet a blue and orange man! Yes,
that is all I need — to meet
        a man with glowing eyes, a man
        with blood-red eyes
                (and yet
                        I am most satisfied to own
                                a dog, who cares for me)

Someday, shall I speak of youth?
or age, which comes upon us
        as a writer to the pen
                In time of famine,
                        all honesty
                                runs silently aground.
Giving of her teat as much
a farmer to the lamb
        Then lets the blow fall,
                silent
                        upon the door of time.

But then I will be young again
The living soul has told me
        How does one begin to die
        without a trace of life?

new york

32

Poem for a Mundane Sermon

It was a topical day in Good Fink George's life. The pun was shining, his roominghouse lovelady took up the rent. All was otherwise a formal state of affairs. The King rose, bumbled down steps, potted with age; made his way to the front whore, opened it, stepped out.

A ram was there complaining as to the rest ban treaty and wondering if there would still be unfound resting. Of course! cried Good Fink George, this will always be! Lady spoke of the surplus new nation problem and he absolved to do something about it immediately.

They set upon him with a mighty roar and ferried him into the castle. Placing a crown of horns upon his head, sitting on the stone in the coroner, they laughed at the Good Fink. He rose the window and raved to the crowd bellow. Outside it was raining fags and dogs. A great fear rolled down his cheek. When the crowd saw the crystal fear they cried Don't spurn the other cheek! and so he didn't.

Making his way backwards, George (the first) began to cry. Upon doing so he felt better and quickly churned aground, spreading his wings long in order to get by them all with their surplus regurgitation problems etc.

It was a topical day in Good Fink George's life.

Dirty Dirty Boy

There's an avenue of people
who believe in faith
And the wanderers suffer
'cause they never get laid
The cause of this injustice
is a world-wide fake

       In lies told to you
       at school
       on the subway
       "Keep your hands in your pockets
       You'll go blind and insane!"

dirty dirty boy
dirty dirty girl
       keep your hands in your pockets
       you'll go blind and insane!

When the lady is a baby
all dressed up to share
She doesn't disappoint you
by playing it fair
She can't shake her money-maker
if it just ain't there
       keep your hands in your pockets
       you'll go blind and insane!

dirty dirty boy
dirty dirty girl
       her mother would say
       Keep your hands in your pockets
       You'll go blind and insane!

new york

By Candlelight In Sullen Night

By candlelight in sullen night
I weave a cloak of dreams
On sea tossed foam I swim alone
None else may touch the seams.
That no one aid me in my quest
Nor interfere with dreams,
I keep my sleeping hours hid
With coverlets unseen.

The portals of my mind
Are opened to those few
Who see my seamstress hands as blind
And realize I know, too.
Me, I cheat on time
By sleeping far too fast
That none may gently wake and find
These dreamer's hands at rest.

I, maker of shrouds,
Should be lone and far away
Wandering through heavy clouds
of angels at their play
Trusting no one but the one
In charge of twilight dreams.
Yet I am keeper and shaker
Of worlds forever, it seems.

> So then. Be quick to snuff a light
> And let the darkness ease your plight.
> Unlovely pen, sketch me a life
> By candlelight in sullen night.

new york

Partly at Paul's

There's a party in the ballroom.
Everybody's got their gowns on
Drinking a toast
to the hostess and host
of the evening.

My friend the armadillo
was wearing all her grease.
The slumming eccentric
went up to see the Priest
who along with Beethoven
was sick, to say the least.

Mister Jones he stood with Lonely
and talked beyond his reach
The sequined Star of yesteryear
stood clicking with her knees.

That's all right, Toulouse-Lautrec,
it's only you and me
Laughing in the doorway at the freaks.

New Christ

New Christ Cardiac Hero
yes, he's very strong
but once it falls
he'll never rise again

Lonely One lurks on my shoulder
clutching teddy bears to his heart
He'd like to sleep with mama
but it's common knowledge she was
dead
before his conception

And Pro-Girl, she's at the door again
It would be easy to buy her
maybe even love her
but I'd only be elevating myself

> Baby's got the blues again
> She's taking off her boots again
> She's climbing into bed again
> She's laying down her head again
> The neighbors think she's frigid
> but it hurts her most of all

Look/Life

Party night back at the old corral. Young superstar Bertha Shlock arrives late (5 min EST) in a flurry of apologies and general talk about lack of sleep due to night work. Then came the introduction, the shaking of cold slimy fish hands but everyone was smiling and so it was O.K. boyo.

Animal Keeper (in charge of looking after superstar's mind and collecting 20% of each nervous breakdown) came with a young man. Of indeterminate age and undefined coloring, he blended into the walls about as well as could be expected.

Hallo SS   he shouted (abbreviated superstar)
Belt up steaming nit   she replied, coughing ectoplasmically. But Bertha baby, here is the reporter from Teen Scream Magazine.

TS: Miss Shlock, does the artist reflect the society around him?

BS: Yah. I'll start mass-producing chaos.

All this was taken down on an eight-track machine, it would later be mixed and sent over to the HUAC Commission on Civil Rights. The HUAC-CCR was concerned at present with the take-over of the Industry by a band of youths calling themselves "Genuine Artists of Creation" who were handled expertly by William Morris agents.

Party night back at the old corral, young superstar Bertha Schlock rapidly succumbing. In the end she was tired but everyone was still smiling so she guessed it was O.K. boyo and then with laughter in her eyes was carried screaming from the room.

new york

My Sullen Song

Standing on your microphone
Yes, I use feedback at times
with no audience reaction
Turn up the volume
(Do they hear me now?)
Turn on some more highs
get rid of the lows

> Then stand, try to laugh
> And the sun calls out
>   fat chance
> So fall, try to cry.
> The river walks by
>   not even staring.

Laugh, go on and drown
Funny isn't it?
how many sessions it takes
before anyone hears the final mix.
You could scratch your eyelids all day
and the tape would run on.

> Then stand, try to sing
> And the wind calls out
>   forever trying
> Fall down, laughter rings
> The sun ambles by
>   not even smiling

And it's a long
     long time
since the last god died

new york

peter

1967

peter

I Love Your Chest Like Cat's Tongue

I love
your chest
like cat's tongue
    ready for the feast
    and also the
fur
like cat's fur
coiled and waiting I love
your hands
like parrot-wings
brushing the dust off
    my corpse
o to be with you
    forever
in our cat's house of
    clay

I love your
ears like
cat's ears
    prickling my
    every sound
    to see your
nails like
cat feet
dart across my back
    dearest but
    most of all I love your
eyes
like cat's eyes
glowing
    after the feast

peter

A Day At the Circus

I

hie, the lonely river
tenement studies in death
manchild, live beneath the sodden earth
surrounded by
the living dead

>Well then dear what **do** you enjoy?

>>*Red-rock sand*
>>*bricks*
>>*the Polynesians...*

summer lay in leisure
gnats upon the pavement
reeking silence

>What's that you say?
>Speak quickly
>I have no time
>The Club awaits me

there are no yesterdays
no future hope
there is only
today
forever

>A child **must** believe in God
>What else can we hold dear?

>>*Red-rock sand*
>>*bricks*
>>*the Polynesians . . .*

don't you see the wind
upon your shoulder
can you see his eyes?
did you hear —
God become a parody

peter

2

ahh
the circus tent
keeps a dream
for many

> oooohhh the snake lady
> writhes in simulated flesh
> Daddy will you buy me
> gee I only wish
> would you buy me
> a cobra, Daddy
> I do so love the snake

He's come at last
with his pointed head
venom full
and beady eyes

> *stand erect*
> *am I yet a child*
> *to cower before Eden?*

Daddy if you buy a snake
my very own
I'll show it to my friends
take it away!
take it away,
Daddy I don't want it anymore!
God   the pain

he's cute
in a funny way
don't come any closer!
please
don't hurt me
O thank you Daddy,
thank you!

> *Deliver me, O God*
> *an easy death*

peter

3

the hunchback dwarf
taps his hands
against the wall
forever

His head
was fragile stalked
grotesque

> *Simon*
> *looked like that*
> *when he was born*

a parody
of God

> *yet three days later*
> *resembled nothing more than*
> *a vacant hole*

but aren't we all?

> don't be scared t' laugh folks
> he can't hear you

> > *Simon*
> > *heard me*

> oh he's been de-manned
> miss
> don't you be afraid, now

> > *Simon*
> > *my son*
> > *was this to be your life?*

4

the fat man
and his coterie
are on parade each day
from noon to twelve
hear before your very eyes
their conversation

> *Haarrryyy she whines*
> *and whines*
> *what manner woman this?*
> *to weigh so little*
> *in the scheme of man*

Think he can shame me?
that hulk
I—I am more beautiful
with my ribs askew
each day
from noon to twelve
it's **me** that draws a crowd

> *surely she must eat*
> *how then does she lose it?*
> *she is gnarled and ugly*
> *and hates me*

Harry!
your shoes
the crowd is laughing

puffing, his hands
scrabble for the earth
and fall backwards
on the ground
hahahahahahaha

> *Am I so ashamed?*
> *to do my laces before you*
> *Ah, the weight of misery*
> *hangs a body low*
> *Stifles the bone sure as*
> *lard*

peter

47

If I had a man
to take me away

> Had I a woman
> fragile as the sea
> to adore

Harry? and me?
you must be kidding ?

> jesus god
> what do you want?
> who would take me as I am
> save her?

what a riot!
did you hear?
they're getting hitched
it's all over town

> She will suck my venom
> She will take my veins
>   and suck the body through
> She will take my livelihood
> out of petty jealousy

Him? he'll be on top
like he's always wanted
and me, I'll be crushed
like as I've always wanted

5

evening
the wedding bells toll
in silence
forever
these are the walls
the walls,
ever pressing down our
fellow man

    Well if you don't like it
    go get somebody else

        Is this the death of hope
        the end of pain?

    Sure, and you bought her
    a snake
    When you know very well
    they scare me to death

        If I'd known then
        all I dare not think of now

    What do you think I am?
     a sewer
     to take your drippings?

        Deliver me, O Lord
        a silent death

    What the hell do you want?

        Red-rock sand
        bricks
        the Polynesians . . .

here we are in summer
the gnats
suffocating a parody of God
from parody
a God

peter

49

This Morning at Sunset

This morning I cried again
(though only with sorrow)
No one
   saw the tears run down
No one
   felt the racking sob
And I alone wept
for all the tears
ever lost in the nap of time

> *There's no fun being in the spotlight*
> *when no one is looking*

This afternoon I screamed
(though only for effect)
No one
   saw my hands upon the rafters
No one
   heard my body shake the walls
And I alone shouted
for all the hands
we let go unnoticed

> *How do you count to ten*
> *if you haven't any fingers?*

This evening I died again
(though only with laughter)
No one
   read my epitaph
No one
   gave black orchids
And I alone
as only I can be
laughed softly through the tears

> *It's no fun dying*
> *if no one sees*

peter

Ambrotype

Politics? o man
you flatter yourself
to venture an opinion
and you're so unready for war
political machinery
you bow and scrape to
all the while the dribble
spills down your chin
clouding your eyes
o man
you flatter yourself to think
even in non-spatial terms
and I wish
you wouldn't impose
your lack of human relations on me

Plasticine Cardboard Cutouts
I came out of the womb
standing when you pressed
tabs A and B
dead I became a piece of earth
and in my furrow of innocence
nourished a maple tree
becoming part thereof
I shielded a rock from rain
and was warm in knowing
it loved me.

carrion of death
wed-winged, soar into the sun
I feel the rising tide within me

> *anger I'll rip you to pieces!*
> *anger I'll scream and shout!*
> *anger we'll make the world over!*

(foolish carrion)
when your wings are dead
from the beat of innocence
can you fly?

peter

when your throat is ripped from the breast
like spawn from the mother lode
will you whisper truths in a monotone?
when the world is made over
will there be room enough
for you to sit still?

bubbling sand
I built a castle by the sea
made of glass

fragile as the wind
and when night rushed in
to take my castle
I was enclosed therein
    picture, if you will
    my being
    carried out to sea
    in a trifling moment
as the castle was rent
the sea
washed my body clean

mr. henry finch esquire III
your sense of righteous indignation
overwhelms me
with your multimillion dollar wife
and your golden pennies children
ashine in fool's gold
you 'deplore the plight of the wretched poor'
mr. henry finch esquire III
your sense of righteous indignation
overwhelms me

sitting in a doorway
you wallowed in degradation
I didn't mean to help you
raise the bottle to your lips!
just wanted to befriend
someone quite as drunk as I—
and share a few memories
I never meant to be you
I only meant to help you
but have I any choice?

death
whose hunger
transforms me
to animal lust
    do not crave my soul
    and leave the body to rot
    in a furrow of steel

I shake my fist at you, death
    for taking what I had
    and returning far less
I spit at you death
    for breaking my nerve
    and leaving the bones

I laugh at you, death
    without the decency
    to capitalize your name
I pray to you
    for taking my soul
    and leaving the knowledge

peter

Analogue

your train
    in
my canyon
    asleep
    on a bed of rails
hurdle
up and down
    I've jumped
    the track
one too many times
    have you been there
    before?
Touch
listen
    your train
    greases
    my rails
smooth riding
    have I been
    before?

The sunset depression
everyone knows
but what of the morning sky?
    my bird
        would fly
            for you

peter

I Am the Lonely River

I

I am the queen of crimson violet blushing
loneliness
and hold the title well
I am the king of black magic
emptiness
(king of satire
ruler of none)
the crown wears easy on my brow
jack of all trades, I am the master sailor
and can fix your vessel in no time
my dear

let the river tell me what I
      already know
that the jack of diamonds is gone
may his shadow hang low
on my brow
as if to mock our sterile setting
calmness runs over.

my cup anointed,
I surrender captain
take me; willingly
I submit

and if they should ask
      what became of her?
      (those foolish wagging tongues)
merely say
I have shrugged my shoulders with the best
of men

peter

II
I am the lonely river
and know no bound'ry
save the shoreline
obedient to the whim of selfish matter
I flow and ebb
consumed by his might
    is this too much to ask of time?
when he beckons
come forth
and on release, sink gently
into my cradle of earth

III
I shall take what I want
and a pox on your revelations!
    (we hear no music, you and I
    but for god's sake
    save the stars)
footloose as I
shoeless as I
the king is dead.

IV
staving hunger
kaleidoscope excels my rate of speed
the shadow moves
too quickly to be seen
    and night
    spent
    raining on my window

peter

It Is Time We Parted

this morning
at dawn
I wakened dead
to all natural resources
the blundering hulk beside me
a burnt out husk
of former affairs

      my friend   said I
      it is time we parted

and he watched with naked eyes
as I packed my bag
and ran for my life
to the home of my wanton lover
my own

Psalms. Psalms

psalms
psalms
hunger is cumulative
and anger contagious
keep away from churches kid

choirs
benches
the old people sit in the park
the young people lie on the grass
keep back from the ages kid

grey
brick
the old buildings are crumbling
the new held together by glue
stick to the middle of the street kid

sun
clouds
the sky being overcast looked at me
I being undercast saw the sun
carry a lightning rod at all times kid

lies
stories
everything they told you was true
and everything they proved was a lie
don't take up metaphysics my boy

laugh
sing
without love where would we be
back in the garden of eden
an apple a day lets you pray boy

so
so
that's the way your life runs
plastic smooth as plastic
don't you think I know kid?

peter

The Arabesque Dancer

Naked in swirls
All bathed in curls
The arabesque dancer wheeled about
and gathered kings
(Such pretty things)
then quickly, shut them out

Her flaming hair
and shoulders bare
have many a man caught unaware
She's captured more
with shining lure
than nature could —
and held them there

> "In the sea I writhe,
> My body bright
> in cold delight of mystery.
> With the sea I cry
> for the pale moonlight
> and morning's eye to comfort me."

There are no words
for what we know
though many men have tried
So may we love
and try to stem
the quickly drowning tide.

Then put no marker on my grave
but leave me with your touch
For the sea I cry
For the ocean, die
and none may say as much

Shed not a tear for you and me—
It can not make us more
and cast a shadow to the waves
The bravest of us all

peter

59

"Accept from me
one fond caress.
For just a moment, stay
and give to me
in tenderness
the blessings of the blessed."

Then stop.
the tragic willow weeps.
And hold me to your breast
for I am the arabesque dancer
and know your loneliness.

So wipe the pity from your eyes
and raise the spuming glass on high
So say to me, my own delight
        "To us, the rising tide."

peter

Bahimsa

When the lilacs of his eyes
turn to chutes of the assassin
and come hurtling down
When the lilies of his youth
turn, fading and brown
When the hourglass of his mind
turns, bleeding and bound
And the roses of his dreams
lie scattered
upon the ground

When the flowers of her lover
have turned to flowers
of the grave
When his caressing lips
have turned from red to grey
When flowers burn, and only
memories remain
His silver medals turned to dust
and an ashen marker
is made

When a wind from Hiroshima
blows ashes
into the town
When they slowly sift to form
a blanket, on the ground
When the earth turns to a tomb
no flowers can be found
And the silken mantle he wore
has turned
into a shroud

peter

Christmas Greetings

and my lover came
on the day of snowbells
sundrifts
moaning in anger

so the evening set
on daily carnival
with laughter flying
over the river

> the morning sun
> did shine upon
> his face
> to laugh
> 'What ecstasy!'
> cried my crippled heart

so in the season of yesteryear
when winter was forever
and tomorrow always today
in the season of mindlessness

so did my latent lover come to me

peter

Like A Lonely Train Wreck, Sneaking

Structured in safety
The poet reeks of hollow song
cutting a heartache
snipping a memory
we have left
    (ta-ta-ta)
your paper doily

       When was I young?
       There were parties.
       Paper doilies.

False poet—
one day per year
acknowledge your birth
    in parties
    Paper doilies

Do you arouse
the women we meet,
and push away their tears?

      I find no grave
      for pain
      Nor final resting place
      with wooden stake
      and paper masque
      It will haunt you
        forever.

Must you be so insipid?
Those afraid to feel
    will buy your name
    will turn the page
       reading aloud to a favorite cat
       buying puppy dogs
         for company

peter

Harbinger of easy love—
I will haunt you forever.
  You mock traditions of the heart!
  You — both blessed and damned.

    A cardboard train
    soot-ridden
    covers the desert
    Is this the only train?
      let us climb aboard
    Rather soot than hunger
      let us climb aboard
    Don't ask when the next train stops!
      rather, climb aboard

Take me for an easy ride —
I will haunt you
    forever.
You are tired
too tired
    Wish me well, fellow muse
    Have I so much time?
Build the bridges high.
Now. Let us surrender.
    Let us buy our cats and dogs
    as we climb aboard

peter

Song of Surrender

I wish I were a snowbird
Sitting in a tree
    laughing wholehearted
    nothing bothers her
    cool as a ruffled pigeon feather
    she flies alone
    no V-formation status symbol here

Veteran of death
loneliness won't save you
    she flies so easy
Wafting through my yesterdays
I found a marker
on the day we killed love
    but better to laugh
    on the day of mourning
    and sing my song to evening
    like a snowbird at twilight
    than spend my days questioning
    the evening silence

peter

The Runes of Atlantis

I see
the city, rising
like a broken vessel
upon the waters of my disbelief

      Mothers who play in the park
      bring children to console themselves
            wait! wait!
            you'll have children too someday!
      go on run around fall down break-a-leg
            hah. then you'll learn

the old men
the dead men
and trees
with gnarled and broken branches
spent, reaching for the sun

      After the red rubber ball, Nicky!
      Catch it quick!
            Ooo you're gonna get it when
            papa finds out . . .

      conditioned fear
      a reflex emotion
      teach your children
      their energy spent
      reaching for the sky

Like a tombstone graveyard
my mind is an inscription
left behind by oblivious corpses
As kings are killed by princes
neverending.

      Zowee cor just look at 'im bleed
      never seen such a sot in m' life

            where's he from
            & what's he done
            forever and for more?

peter

your children learn in school
when you kill the power
for the throne
beware!
and stop your brother's moan

the young girls
carelessly sun themselves
young boys
carelessly intrude
spinning mad circles
through destiny

but I can not love their jellied limbs
broken, in careless ecstasy
I can not love their withered smiles
nor can I grieve for this my own
laid out before the sun

> Oh my God
> Is it so ugly
> to have tried and failed?
>> *no one comes near you*
>> *ever again*

for countless prisons have I wrung
the sweat, in beads
from off my tongue
of too much bitterness installed
too much pain
and too much gall

> So laugh! the park
> is filled with trees
> and let the silent mourners file
> slowly past
> Children, come!
> join in the play!
>> *you'll die to dance*
>> *another day*

peter

67

What Then, Eurydice?

I
And if I should die before you sleep
What then, Eurydice?
Will you force a tear down the ridge
to please me
as I lie there, teasing you with life?
Bend low to hear my gasping breath
shortened at last
by space
  Infinity
  has always been my name

II
Solder the coffin tight, mother.
Don't forget —
  we have a habit to maintain
Bury the dead without your grief
They cannot hear.
  Only a till of sod in life
  I am the living sky

III
Don't let the children
call my name in their sleep
I fear it will wake you
God knows
we tried hard enough
to teach you life
  Sleep.
  Your dark imprisonment
  comes too soon before the light

IV
Be not ashamed, Eurydice
  for the sky to carry my longing.
Be not ashamed, Eurydice
  of the lonely stranger
  death

peter

unpublished

1968

Atthis

In the wine red sea, my treasure,
there is a hollow
where the sun never shows his face

I've dreamed it often enough
thinking of you

When I see you
at the center
of an ocean too deep to admit,
I can taste safe harbor
brushing against my face
blowing against your hair
pushing us out to sea

Atthis, my mouth
is wet
with longing

I Was Only Standing There

I was just standing there
minding my own business
if it can be called business
when a white lady in pink florals approached
consternation on her face

"You're the girl who sings that song"
she informed me

I relaxed then
waiting for the compliments
but she spit full in my face
then walked away
with a contented smile

How humiliating to think
that my entire life history
can be summed up in a stranger's saliva

When I thought of giving an audience pleasure
I didn't imagine it would be like this

Billie's Bones

I
I stand on the bones of my elders.
I walk on the carcasses of those
who went before me
Billie is my idol, I
wander through the desert
of her later years
      copying every bleached bone
      mimicking each tattered muscle
      watching for any sign of life
      trying to grin with the ease of
      her skull, grinning back at me
And all I've learned
from all this desert
is just how well I fail

II
I despair of ever singing
with the truth
her naked skull conveys
I spend so much time with corpses
that my breath reeks of carrion
When the wind blows right
you can taste me coming

III
These layers of extra fat
have got to go
They're in the way of the bones
and nothing
speaks louder
than the bones

IV
If anyone wants to know
what I make of my poor efforts
tell them I am ash
dust on the wind
and I have no tongue

unpublished

Our First Abortive Date

If I could speak the way you spoke
when you spoke to me that way
I would have said
"How dare you?
"Don't you remember who I am?
"Can't you see who I want to be?"

How can your tolerance be so low?
and how can you
of all people
misread me this way?

My hands hunger
for the touch of you
and all you want to feel
is dust

My mouth
hungers
for the taste of you
and all you want to eat
is ash

If I could speak the way you spoke
when you spoke to me that way
I would be crippled by shame
but you, apparently,
have no such excuse

unpublished

Sailor Suits & Crinolines

I do not like
little boys in sailor suits
with shiny brass buttons
and bleached white socks

I despise little girls
in white crinolined dresses
whose black patent leather shoes
reflect everything upwards
like some Catholic school teenager's dream

If we all dressed that way
how would we know
who our friends are?

11–15–66

A New Translation of the Old Testament

1. In the beginning there was a new god, there was the god of the Jews, the one and mighty god. And the Jews looked and saw that this new God was not Baal, who seethed kids in their mother's milk for battle feasts. That made them happy.

2. Then God their God said "I am a jealous God." And the Jews fell back in fear. But they continued in their transgressions. That made God unhappy.

3. So their god went and fought the various other gods, gods of the Incas & the Aztecs & the Toltecs & the Medomins & the Seconals. It was a mighty thing that fight, and the world was wiped clean once more. That made everyone who survived happy.

4. And the god of the Indians was not happy, so he urinated for 40 days and nights and made a mighty flood. And the Indians looked and saw the flood was good, as it wiped out most of the rest of humanity. And the world was clean again, at least, in their little corner of it.

5. Then they wrote the book on Eden, where Adam and Eve had a son named Harvey who thought he was a rabbit. God despaired.

6. Came the Tower of Babel, where Harvey got a job making boxes. Eve, meanwhile, was kept busy entertaining the snakes and later became a professional fight manager.

7. Absalom fell in love with his father's girlfriend, who saw nothing wrong with it. The rest of the family, however, disagreed.

8. Eventually came Christ, preaching Indian mysticism He had learned during His exile in the East. (Or West, as the case may be and depending on where you lived at the time.) And His followers were known as the Nazarenes, or Followers of That Guy from Nazareth. And they did promise, after the death of their Christ, to observe the Jewish ways, and thus it continued for a while. But not for long enough.

9. Then came Paul, who was Saul but took a stage name, who was blind and then could see. And he said he saw a vision of Christ the Saviour, also known as Jesus, or That Kid From Down the Block Who Gets All the Cute Girls.

10. And Paul, also known as Saul, who was a braggart and a thief and a charlatan, said to the dying Roman empire "I have seen Jesus and converted, look at me! Look at me!" And some looked and thought this was good.

11. And Paul, who had never seen Christ In the Flesh, but only In the Spirit and with his inner eye (remember he had been blind until then, who are we to judge?), said "LO, I have had a revelation. Now it will be easy to be a Christian. Before, you had to become circumcised. Before, you had to obey the Law, and know how to read. Now, all we need is faith."

12. And the lazy folk listened and saw it was good. And followed.

13. Then the Christ-ians, for such were the followers of Paul, promised to help the Jews in their revolt against the Romans, for the Romans were verily enemies of the Christ-ians as well. And so the Jews planned a mighty revolt, which with the help of the Christ-ians they believed to win, for their numbers would be many.

14. And on the appointed day the Jews revolted, and waited in the hills for their compatriots the Christians, who had decided to take a mental

unpublished

health day and did not show.

15. Thus was the Temple of Solomon destroyed. Thus did the Christ-ians, being martyred up until then, make themselves able to say "Yes we are martyrs, we are the lowest of the low, but look ye, for the Jews are yet lower." And thus did the Romans, and then the Christians, slaughter the Jews with impunity.

16. And thousands of years later a man named Hitler came forth, and since the Holy Roman Church had always held the Jews liable for the death of Christ their leader, he was able to enlist the aid of many of them as he set about killing all the Jews. And no one in the papacy cried out. And everyone stood by as the Jews were slaughtered, women, children, grandma and grandpa too. And they thought "Yuck, the means might be questionable, but on the whole, what a guy!." And the earth was cleansed again.

17. Years later an enlightened Pope made this announcement.
   a) "Lo and behold, the Jews are not guilty of killing Our Saviour,
   b) who went to his death willingly and would not have us cast stones.
   c) Eek!
   d) We should stop torturing them."

And all the Jews of the world heaved a mighty sigh of relief.

18. Then they killed the Pope. Of course.

19. What did you expect?

20. It is hard to be a Jew, but it's harder to be a cockroach. Everybody knows that.

unpublished

Relativity In Motion

Now they talk about time being relative
and all that
but I say

> who'd want to make a cousin of
> something
> that just kills you in the end?

We are droning Spanish infinitives
hablo, hablas, hablan
hablamos, habláis, hablaran
while the teacher picks her cuticles

> Why doubt the existence of black
> holes
> when they're right here for all to
> see?

They can put a man on the moon
but they can't manage to put
decent schools in the city

> Go figure

When they talk about relativity
I wonder if any of these teachers
are the product of

> first cousins
> marrying

I Read Sappho Before She Was Cool

I read Sappho before she was cool
Now it's trendy
to bill and coo over Mary Renault
but I still remember ordering
sly girl-books
from catalogues I picked up
on a Village street
behind my parent's backs

> You are so very pretty
> dare I say
> or would handsome be better,
> though less informed?

I am not one for sentiment
Noble trees in the mist,
happy starlings at dawn,
they leave me cold
I have enough trouble
with my own rude desire

unpublished

Hate Mail in the Mail

I get hate mail in the mail
courtesy the US Postal Service
always on time
diligent as a mobster on assignment

The postman grins, he brings the bag
too heavy for me
and puts it on Jean's coffee table
"Guess you're really famous now"
he tells me with a wink
"All this fan mail. Must feel good
for a little girl like you
to have so many friends."

They chat and smile
while I stare at the bag
wondering how many bombs
it will hold today

I am not little I am
just a girl who sings
and if one of these packages explodes
it will blow off your fingers too

unpublished

You Are Too Cute For Words (for Pat)

you are
too cute
for words

the way your
eyes swing
back and forth
when no one's looking

the way your hair
softens the pillow
as you sleep
unintended

i think sometimes
i am the luckiest person on earth
but then i realize
there's a universe out there
and it's filled
with your grace

if i were
a poet
i would fill
every rose
with you

May 2000

Afterword

Well, there you have it. The childhood and adolescent ramblings of a gifted writer with a propensity for too much verbiage.

When I announced plans to reissue *Who Really Cares*, my website was inundated with emails from fans wanting to know "the stories behind the poems." Since I spend a good portion of my live show talking about "the stories behind the songs," it seemed a good idea to provide some sort of key with this book. (Particularly since we are now several generations past the '60s counterculture, and many people reading this won't know the reference points.)

Remember that these poems were written between 1961 and 1967, a time of great change in America. Those years are increasingly difficult to explain to generations who've grown up *knowing* that women are as smart as men, blacks are not inherently inferior, and every adult in America has the right to vote. These were not givens when I was growing up.

Imagine how hard it is for today's fifteen-year-old to picture that world. No videos, microwaves, or remote controls. No Internet, computers, or faxes. The only instant communication was by telephone, and all telephones (as well as telephone services) were owned by one giant company that kept prices high and services low. Calling another state, let alone overseas, was too prohibitive for anything less than a life and death emergency.

Air conditioning was only for the very rich. People in wheelchairs were hidden away by their embarrassed families. There was no FM radio, no shopping mall, no disposable lighter in existence. We had no synthesizers, let alone home-recording studios — the transistor radio was cutting edge technology. Hotels routinely refused to admit Jews, or blacks, or in some cases even actors. And it was legal to do so!

It is immensely difficult, now, to envision an

America where gay people were routinely institution-alized and given lobotomies and shock treatment to "treat their illness." Where it was illegal for women to wear "men's clothing" (pants and flat shoes) in some public places. Where husbands were not allowed in delivery rooms, and children could never visit their hospitalized mothers.

Imagine a world where the only working people on television are white males, and everyone wears a suit to work. Where there are, literally, *no* black people on TV. And where a family like mine can be kept under sur-veillance by the FBI for two decades because my father (a farmer at the time) attended a meeting about the price of eggs!

It's hard to conceive, even for me. How much more difficult, then, for someone several generations removed.

The young women of today take their checking accounts and credit cards for granted, rarely realizing that a scant two generations ago, women could only have those things with a husband's name on them. Married women keep their maiden names, something that was unthinkable (and often not possible) then. Divorcées are permitted to rent apartments, single mothers are allowed to enroll their children in local schools, and a child born out of wedlock is no longer a pariah.

The world is very different for men now, too. In my childhood, males were not allowed to cry — it wasn't "manly." Nor were they encouraged to speak about their feelings (or even admit to having them). Men were sneered at if they spent too much time with their chil-dren; many men from my parents' and grandparents' generation missed the simple joys a child can bring, because they weren't *supposed* to diaper, feed, or bathe their children. That was women's work, and it was demeaning if a man did it.

Men didn't choose furniture, or wall paint colors, or

even their own clothing. Women did that. Men chose cars, then had to know how to fix them. A man who didn't mow his own lawn was considered shiftless; a woman who mowed was pitiable. The world was divided by gender, by color, by religion.

Then came the sixties, when we tried to blow up the past. And in many ways, succeeded.

You want to know why we rebelled? *Because it was stifling.* It was impossible to breath. All over this nation, children and adolescents of my generation were feeling the same thing. We did not want the safe, secure world of our parents — we wanted more. We wanted truth, and justice, and liberty. We demanded what we'd been promised, and when the system failed to deliver it, we tried to make it happen anyway. This wasn't only being felt by small groups of radicals — it was omnipresent.

And once FM radio began, tying us together through music, a revolution of sorts was inevitable.

Chief among the changes wrought by the sixties were ease of transportation, and the rise of television. When I was born, owning a TV was a rarity. By the time I hit twenty-one, it was the norm. Television and transportation shrank our world. They allowed us to experience how people in other states and countries lived; to perceive them as human beings, with all the frailties and strengths we expected in our neighbors. When blacks began appearing on television, many whites suddenly saw them as fellow citizens, rather than strangers from an alien culture. To see a man like Sidney Poitier, eloquent and elegant, was a great surprise to many people in this country.

TV appearances humanized us to one another, doing a great deal to erase people's bigotry and fear. Whatever your outcast status — black, an actor, a performer, Hispanic, Irish, gay, an unwed mother, a stay-at-home father — television portrayed you at some point in the '60s, and America saw you as a neighbor, not a threat. Regional differences began to be erased. As we watched peaceful civil rights marchers attacked with billy clubs and water hoses, formerly complacent viewers suddenly realized that there was something terribly wrong with the way large portions of this country treated some of its citizens. The civil rights movement was no longer something "they" were doing. It was *here*, right in our living rooms.

I miss a lot of things about those days. There was a sense of excitement in the air that I haven't seen duplicated since. We thrived on it, on the transformation we saw happening around us.

Television in the sixties was *fun*, in the worst possible way. I raced home after school to watch coverage of John Kennedy's assassination, and saw Lee Harvey Oswald shot to death live on national TV. I watched Kent State happen, and read in the next day's paper the government lie: *There were snipers on the roofs, that's why the National Guard shot those students.* I saw the Chicago Seven on trial, and watched the riots in that city, a bloody manifesto of the old guard brutally supressing the new. I saw Martin Luther King marching in Selma, and Nixon denying Watergate. In between, I saw the Beatles on Ed Sullivan, and clapped for Peter Pan and Tinkerbell. With only seven channels available, and live TV the norm, it was never dull.

I took my first plane trip in 1966, at the age of fifteen. Even then, women wore dresses and gloves on airplanes. Heck, we got dressed up to go to the movies! And it *was* stultifying. Putting a suit and tie on for work, only to change into mechanic's overalls once you got there, was just plain silly. Not being allowed into a restaurant because you were a female in pants was silly. Watching American boys die in Viet Nam when there wasn't a prayer of winning was ignorant, savage, American *hubris* at its worst.

My generation was brought up to believe that the government always told the truth, marijuana made you insane, and all parents loved and protected their children. Nice women weren't interested in sex, and they certainly didn't have orgasms the way men did. America was infallible, opportunity was open to everyone, and anyone could grow up to be president. I'm not making this up — this is what we were taught — in the schools, in the papers, in our homes.

Watergate. Viet Nam. Marijuana. Statistics on child abuse and incest. J. Edgar Hoover keeping files on everyone and anyone, threatening them with black-mail until the day he died. The government railing against drugs, then manufacturing LSD and dousing countless unknowing GI's, let alone civilians, in their search for the ultimate truth drug. *The Joy of Sex* and the Masters & Johnson reports. Most of all, our own impatience with a world we found too slow, and too satisfied with the way things were. All of that con-spired to blow everything we'd been taught out the window.

And once we found out how much the govern-ment and teachers lied, it was a short leap to believe that *all* adults lied. Even the well-meaning ones.

The poetry you've just read was written against the backdrop of the sixties, a mural splashed with the portraits of tens of thousands of "children" who want-ed nothing more than to make a better, safer world for themselves and the future. We are in that future now.

BACKGROUND NOTES

PAGE 3: *Poems for the Young Bedwetter* — I wrote this series (*Poems for the Young Psychologist/Bedwetter/Guidance Counselor*) when I was 12 or 13. I have a brother, 3½ years younger than I am, who is one of the great joys in my life. But I'd also gotten a couple of psychology books out of the library, and thought that writing truthfully about things I would never say out loud might be fun.

PAGE 4: *Horatio* —— We lived near Needle Park in New York, the nickname coming from the immense number of addicts and dealers who frequented that small patch of greenery. It was fascinating to watch junkies, bums, religious fanatics, hookers, and Boy Scouts, all occasionally sharing the same space and doing a pretty good job of ignoring one another.

PAGE 5: *The Droning Rebels* — Just a series of *vignettes*, random thoughts and memories. "home james politicians" was a slam at the conservative politicos who imitated the English upper class. The "Madison Ave. boys spineless mindless lads" were the hordes of men I'd see going to work at advertising agencies every day, wearing identical suits and ties, carrying identical briefcases, and probably keeping identical wives and children somewhere at home.

PAGE 8: *79th Street* was seven blocks from my parent's apartment. The pool hall employed an elderly black man who fetched and carried everything from coffee to chalk.

PAGE 12: *Cock Robin is Dead* — As I said previously, I was entranced with death. It seemed very romantic, so though I hadn't known Richard Fariña well, I wrote about him. This is humiliating to admit, but there you have it.

PAGE 13: *Poem for the Christening* — What if Jesus had been born in the fifties, lived in the Bronx and had to get Bar Mitzvah'd? This would have made a better story than it is a poem.

PAGE 14: *Philo Judaeus* was an Alexandrian Jew who lived from 20 BC to about 50 AD. He headed a grievance mission that confronted Caligula, so I considered him pretty upright and brave. Just think of the changes he saw during his lifetime!

PAGE 15: *Mandy In Mourning* — When I first began singing in public, I begged for gigs, and wound up at a lot of hospitals and nursing homes. Mandy was a sweet, semi-catatonic girl who lived in one.

PAGE 18: *With His Crazy Black Hair, Whistling A Breeze* — Unlike Richard, I had known Peter LaFarge, and liked him very, very much. This was written for him.

PAGE 19: *Mama & me* — My poor mom . . . when I think of all I put her through, I cringe. My resentment at her insistence that I stay in school when I could be performing or recording, my determination to live my own life rather than anything she wanted for me, found its way into poems. Fortunately for me, after much heartache and a fair amount of therapy on both sides, we became best friends, and I had decades of her love and support to sustain me thereafter.

PAGE 25: *Shaving the Turkey* — One of the basic insults of that era was to call a person a "turkey"; it implied stupidity, but it also meant you were setting yourself up to become someone's next Thanksgiving meal. "Thirsty Boots" refers to a song by Eric Anderson.

PAGE 29: *Eugene the Crazyboy* — My parents ran a summer camp which advertised itself as *Interracial, Multicultural* long before such things were acceptable. The camp was also the subject of ongoing FBI investigations (sample from one report: *With binoculars, observed white and Negro children playing together*). A leak culminated in the headline "Commie camp discovered in upstate New York!" by the ever-inflammatory *New York Daily News*. The headline resulted in a fringe right-wing group called The Minutemen planting bombs in the children's section. (Which had to be dismantled by the FBI to ensure the campers' safety. Life is full of such ironies.) Eugene was a camper, and he truly was not well. Completely disconnected from most of the days' events, he was content to spend most of his time humming. For some reason, though, we struck up a friendshp of sorts.

PAGE 30: *Hunter* — I was close friends with a wonderful guitarist named Carol Hunter, and wrote this for her. She was appalled.

PAGE 34: *Dirty Dirty Boy* — During the '60s, frank discussions of sexuality between males and females forced the stripping away of layers of lies. Yes, they really did tell people "If you masturbate, you'll go blind and insane." And hair would grow on your palms. Yeah, right.

PAGE 35: *By Candlelight In Sullen Night* — Well, I'd just discovered Dylan Thomas.

PAGE 36: *Partly at Paul's* — Paul Marshall was a noted entertainment lawyer who also consulted with various small nations as a legal advisor. Rumor had it he'd actually authored the charter of the Dominican Republic. I don't know whether that's true, but to be invited to one of his parties meant you were about as hip as you could get. The only problem for me was that I was never hip, and going to a party full of "cool" people was uncomfortable at best. Their clothing, their conversation points, their very easiness among all that wealth seemed suspect to me. The people I considered "cool" were much too busy saving the world to go to parties. . . .

"The armadillo" was an actress who'd had so many facelifts that I imagined her fascial layers would resemble an armadillo; the "slumming eccentric" was a beat poet conversing with Allen Ginsberg and Lucian Berio in a corner. Dylan was there, with his coterie, and an anorexic aging star of screen. I can't remember who Toulouse-Lautrec really was; probably an imaginary friend I'd brought along for company.

PAGE 37: *New Christ* — I have no idea where the song "New Christ Cardiac Hero" came from, or why I chose that image. If I try to break it down, I imagine I was referring to the "new" Christ, the one we were all searching for amidst the rubble of organized religion. And of course, he would be the hero of our hearts, once found. "Lonely One" refers to the performer in one of my songs; "Pro-Girl" the kind-hearted whore in another.

PAGE 38: *Look/Life* — To get into *Look* or *Life Magazine* was considered the pinnacle of fame, so when each did a long spread on me, I became very trendy. This is my take on another party, where the press courted me and my manager tried to keep a lid on my mouth.

PAGE 44: *A Day At the Circus* — This is a difficult poem for me, because it failed. My imagination was way beyond my scope and talent at that time. I envisaged it as an internal conversation between three people, none of whom had any idea what the other was thinking. The first would be the moderator, who would shift persona depending on the circumstance. The second was to be "the common man," at his most degraded. And the last would be me, or the person the common man was speaking with. So I began, in section one, with my own reflection on the Hudson River, surrounded by apartments filled with dull people. I inserted a wealthy mother speaking sharply to her questioning child, and that child's unspoken thoughts in answer.

In part two, I drew on my backstage experience at the circus when I was about four. We lived in Farmingdale New Jersey, and every year we had a real, old fashioned circus, complete with sweaty tent, sticky sawdust, and a freak show. The interaction between the freaks themselves, and the freaks with their audience, fascinated me. A little girl kept demanding that her father buy her a pet snake, long a phallic symbol in psychological literature. The parents were terribly uncomfortable around the Snake Lady, and I imagined the father's thoughts in response to her demands.

In part three, I'd watched a woman staring at the hunchbacked dwarf in the show, and wondered if she'd given birth to such a child. I wondered how it would hurt her, to hear the pitchman's spiel.

In four, the fat man and his skinny wife were having

an argument, loud and clear, as they marched around the circus ring.

In five, I went back to the girl who wanted a pet snake, and imagined her parent's conversation after, as each reflects on their marriage. I then tried desperately to tie it all together, and as I said, it failed.

PAGE 51: *Ambrotype* — Webster's Dictionary defines this as " a positive picture made of a photographic negative on glass backed by a dark surface." Go figure.

PAGE 57: *It Is Time We Parted* — As I approached my 17th birthday, I was beginning to wonder about this fame thing. I'd wanted to be famous a long time, but I also wanted a life as a writer. It didn't seem I could have both. I began thinking of leaving the famous part behind.

PAGE 58: *Psalms, Psalms* — People were constantly asking me for advice; should they become a singer? a writer? a priest? This was the best I could do for them.

PAGE 61: *Bahimsa* — I had a number of Buddhist friends who used the word "Ahimsa" (Hindu for kindness to all life, I believe) and the phrase "B'ahimsa" a lot. This poem, which became a song, was based on a series of pictures taken at Hiroshima after the bomb.

PAGE 63: *Like A Lonely Train Wreck, Sneaking* — This was my shout of rage at every false poet I'd encountered. Some of them, as it turned out, were not so false; they were only limited by their lack of talent. But I was pretty elitist about such things, even then.

PAGE 66: *The Runes of Atlantis* — I went through a period of being fascinated by Edgar Cayce, particularly his health readings and remedies. That led me to his readings on Atlantis, and I wanted to "explore" a series of past lives, from Shakespeare to Updike. (It didn't matter to me that John Updike was very much alive; I imagined him in the past anyway.) Another failure.

PAGE 68: *What Then, Eurydice?* — Gosh, for someone who never finished 10th grade, I certainly knew a lot of esoteric references. She was the lover of Orpheus, who descended into hell to bring her back to earth. I loved the film *Black Orpheus*, probably saw it a dozen times before writing this.

PAGE 71: *Atthis* — I'd run across some fragments of Sappho's poetry, quoted in another book I was reading. Her economy of words and motion fascinated me, the way she could speak volumes with a few lines. Her sensuality of line still enthralls. When I submitted this as part of the book, it was suggested that since Atthis was a Greek female's name, it would not be "appropriate."

PAGE 72: *I Was Only Standing There* — Another take on the joys of fame.

PAGE 73: *Billie's Bones* — A major problem with fame at an early age is that you know you're a fraud. It didn't matter what the reviewers said; I *knew* I wasn't a great singer. Or writer. Or performer. I hoped to be, but in the meantime, I was trading on sheer talent. One of the most profound things anyone ever said to me was when Stella Adler told me "Ah, my dear. You have reached the age where talent is no longer enough."

I was focused, to be sure; when I was twelve and someone explained how important breathing through the diaphragm was for a singer, I went to bed each night for a year counting out two hundred diaphragm breaths before I'd allow myself to fall asleep. (I figured it would eventually become habit, and it did.) But outside of rudimentary piano lessons and voice training, I was on my own.

I discovered Billie Holiday when I was 15 or 16 and Herb Gart gave me a set of her albums. From the first note, I hungered for her voice. I made it my goal to rise to the level she'd attained. To sing from the truth, instead of from the craft, is something I've searched for ever since. We singers are limited by the instruments of our birth, but if you listen to my first album, then listen to *Stars*, you'll see just what a profound effect she had on me. Even now, when I feel like my vocals are getting off track, I put Billie on for a few days, and I'm right back where I need to be.

I don't know why the publishers didn't like this poem; it was one of the truer things I wrote. Perhaps the idea of a teen idol saying "All I've learned... is just how well I fail" was too much. In those days, your image was closely guarded, even when you didn't want one.

PAGE 74: *Our First Abortive Date* — Isn't it just about the worst thing in the world, to be an adolescent asking someone for a date, and be turned down with cruelty?

PAGE 75: *Sailor Suits & Crinolines* — Yes, people dressed their children that way. Yuck.

PAGE 76: *A New Translation of the Old Testament* — We moved a lot, the result of my father's inability to attain tenure when he became a teacher because of the ongoing FBI investigation. Oddly enough, though we were Jews, we never lived in a "Jewish neighborhood." Instead, I grew up as an outsider in neighborhoods that were predominantly black Baptist, or Puerto Rican Catholic, or white Protestant and Catholic. Of all the religions I encountered, Catholicism seemed the strangest. I could enter their churches, but they weren't allowed in a synagogue. They couldn't go to certain movies. They had to take after-school classes in something called Catechism (which I imagined to be a course in Catholic table manners), and play with beads (at one point I thought about converting, just to get my hands on all the *accoutrements*). Most of all, they had what I considered to be a very strange interpretation of the Bible. None of my Catholic friends realized that Jesus was Jewish, and didn't believe me when I insisted it was true. Worse yet, they blamed *us* for Jesus' death. I remember my relatives rejoicing when a papal encyclical (or perhaps decree? I get confused) said we had not been responsible. My older relatives had seen their families butchered by Cossacks waving crosses before them. It was hoped that with the Pope's declaration, a lot of the tacit encouragement of anti-Semitism would cease. Of course, that Pope died suddenly and was never autopsied. We have not seen his like since.

PAGE 79: *Relativity In Motion* — That's how I spent my school days, writing poetry and songs. Sort of like I spend my days now, only younger.